CW00431008

CONTENTS

PUBLISHED BY THE MIDHURST SOCIETY 2021
President: Philip Jackson | Chair: Mike Balmforth | Editor: Harvey Tordoff

DISCOVER. FOLLOW. SHARE.
midhurstsociety.org.uk | Facebook and Instagram: @themidhurstsociety

FRONT COVER PHOTO: Cecil Gilbert

Designed and typeset by HOOLI.

EDITOR'S FOREWORD

By Harvey Tordoff

This memoir is of interest not just to people who know Stedham, and will no doubt recognize names and places. It is an important piece of social history, depicting life in rural England before the Great War.

The Midhurst Society was established as a guardian of Midhurst Rural District. We seek to protect our historic buildings and preserve our culture. To that end, we have published magazines, leaflets, and a number of books. We attach particular importance to recording personal memories, because they are unique and otherwise will be lost.

In October 2020 we were approached by Richard Gilbert. He thought we might be interested in a memoir written by his grandfather, Cecil Gilbert, describing his childhood in Stedham in the early part of the 20th century. Richard shared the memoir with us, and we realized immediately that it was definitely worth preserving.

It wasn't quite long enough for a book and we pondered serializing it in our bi-annual magazine, but we felt that it deserved to be published intact, not piecemeal over two or three years. We had recently revised the format of our magazine, and decided that this format would work if we treated the memoir as a special issue. We suggested this to Richard and he agreed.

We typed up the text exactly as Cecil had written it. We made no attempt at editing, we wanted Cecil's voice to speak to us across the years, complete with colloquialisms and imprecise grammar, although we did change the order. Cecil had darted about and repeated himself, and it appeared to be written over a number of sessions. We streamlined it slightly into recognizable chapters. Otherwise, this is a reasonably accurate reminiscence of an old Stedham man.

There was an added bonus. Cecil had made a number of sketches, showing Stedham scenes as he remembered them. We have included them, along with a number of views – historic and current.

We hope that you are as enchanted as we were.

Harvey

Harvey Tordoff, Editor, The Midhurst Society

Acknowledgements: I would like to thank the Gilbert family for allowing us to make public this very personal archive. Thanks also to Reg Symonds, Society member and Stedham man, for taking me on a walking tour of the village identifying scenes from Cecil's memoir.

PREFACE

By Cecil Gilbert

As I am writing this, in my mind I seem to be travelling on a long journey and the train is thought. I enjoy every minute of it, but the time passes very quickly and then the clock strikes and so I realise it is time to go to bed.

There are two reasons why I am putting pen to paper. The first is to give my children's children some idea of what life was actually like when I was a boy. The second was to turn my mind from the loss and sadness of my dear wife's death, to long past happy memories which date back to 1907. They are most factual with may be just a little dash of fiction.

C. E. G. Gilbert
1899-1992

Cecil and Elsie

WHERE THE AUTHOR WAS BORN

AND IN THE EARLY MORNING A LITTLE RED SQUIREEL WOULD SIT ON THE FENCE NIBBLEING NUTS

INTRODUCTION

TO THE MEMORY OF DEAREST ELSIE

I commenced writing this book in 1977, but quite recently my darling wife has passed away, also a brother, so now I'm all alone at 84 years old with just my memories, and happy memories they are; they reach back to the time when I was five years old.

I was the eldest of four boys, although one died when he was eighteen months old. My father and his two brothers had a workshop in the village. They were carpenters by trade. Like a good many other villagers in England some turned their hands to blacksmithing, undertaking, painting and house decorating, my father and uncles did all of these. I used to love to go to the workshop on Saturday mornings to see my eldest uncle - as the eldest he was the 'boss', of course, and he did the paying out. He used to carry the money to the workshop in a little hessian bag and turn it all out onto one of the benches. At this time there were four men employed, and an apprentice. Each had a little black note book in which they entered the job they were doing and the time showing how long each job took (the hours were entered by the side). This Time Book was then handed to my uncle. Starting with the eldest employee, right down to the apprentice (who came last), he reckoned up the hours and paid each man according to his rate of pay - no envelopes to put the money in, but just gave them the cash in their hands. They all seemed to go home satisfied with their pay.

When all the workers had gone my uncle would get a broom and sweep up the shavings off the floor, onto a heap in the corner. Sometimes he would fill a bag with some shavings to take home to start the kitchen fire the next morning; and so the workshop was locked up. We always used to wait for our father and uncle to go home with them, but during the plum season uncle would help us to hunt around near the shop door for greengages, as there was an old greengage tree which every year would bear luscious fruit.

Uncle would say 'Don't eat too many and spoil your dinner'. 'And mind you don't get a wasp in your mouth, as they hang on to the greengages pretty tight unless they've eaten well, and then they drop out of the fruit drunk with juice.' And so Saturday morning at the workshop ended. However, my uncle was always there again, sharp at 8 o'clock on Monday morning to see if the workmen were there on time!

Our father and mother were good parents to us, and did their best to bring us up to be respectable citizens. We always had to

Stedham Church

F. J. NEWMAN.

10 The Street or as it used to be known, No. 10 Stedham.

be punctual at meals, and always had to say the Grace, which father would finish by saying Amen.

On Sundays we had to dress in our best clothes and behave ourselves: I well remember rebelling because we had to go to Sunday school at 9.30 am, then Matins at 11 am, and Children's Service at 3 o'clock. On Sunday afternoon we would go for a walk over the Common, usually with both parents, but if our mother was tired she would stay home and rest. Most Sunday evenings we would spend around the fire, (that was in the winter) and mother would play the piano and father the violin; it was, of course, hymns or sacred songs and solos. Mother had a good, sweet voice, and we

As I am writing this, in my mind I seem to be travelling on a long journey and the train is thought. I enjoy every minute of it, but time passes very quickly.

boys were expected to join in. Later in life I 1earned to play the piano, and when our parents had grown old, before I left them to go across the road to my own home, father always wanted me to play the hymn 'Abide with Me'. I got so used to playing it I could always sit down and play it without the music. Happy days they were too.

School days for me weren't particularly happy. I was slow in picking up things and shocking at arithmetic - not so my brothers, they seemed to get well ahead of me, by passing out and going to the Grammar school. They were later apprenticed to the printing trade. However, when I left school, father thought I ought to go in for wheelwrighting, which I did. I found it very interesting, but jolly hard work.

GILBERT
FAMILY TREE

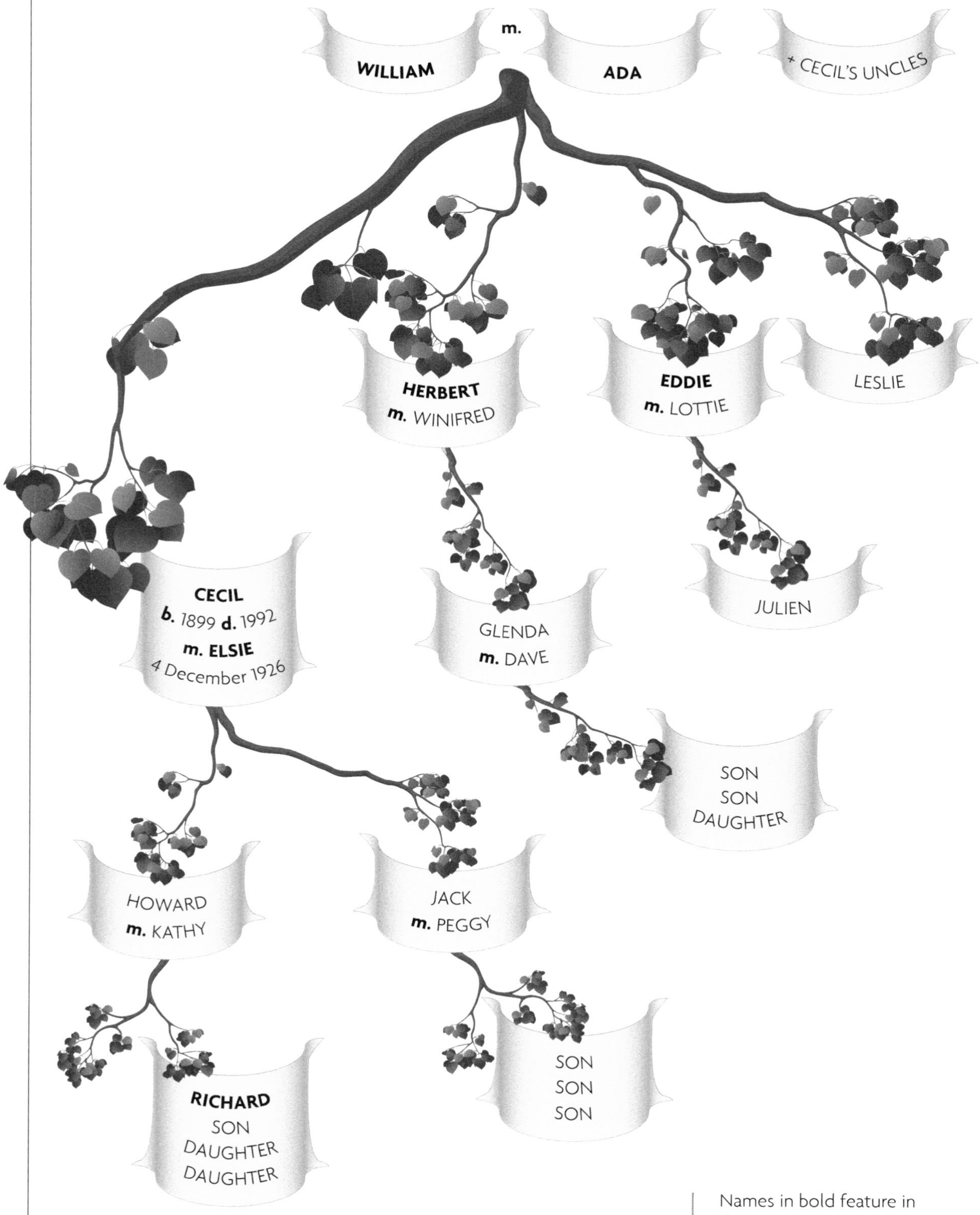

WILLIAM **m.** **ADA** + CECIL'S UNCLES

HERBERT **m.** WINIFRED

EDDIE **m.** LOTTIE

LESLIE

CECIL
b. 1899 **d.** 1992
m. ELSIE
4 December 1926

GLENDA **m.** DAVE

JULIEN

SON
SON
DAUGHTER

HOWARD **m.** KATHY

JACK **m.** PEGGY

RICHARD
SON
DAUGHTER
DAUGHTER

SON
SON
SON

Names in bold feature in this document.

The old workman, whose brother was the boss, made me plane up the rough felloes, (that is the outer sections of the wheel) and they were of curly grained oak; and when I first started this job, by the end of the day my arms ached so much I could hardly hold up the plane. Another job I had to do was to auger out the stock (or the centre barrel shaped piece of wood into which the spokes were mounted). 'Keep the auger straight, boy', I was continually being told, and so I had to do just that. My hours were from 8 am until 5.30 p.m., with an hour for dinner. My pay was half-a-crown a week and my place of work was three miles from my home. Father bought me an old second-hand ladies bike, with only one brake, which was pressed down on the tyre, and a fixed wheel at that! 'Now you're earning a bit,' he said, 'You can buy yourself a bell and a lamp'. A lamp was right! Firstly, I bought an oil lamp, which used to smoke like a chimney and I had to get off the bike to clean the glass, otherwise it was all smoked up and I couldn't see where I was going, or else if it was a windy night it would keep blowing out! After that I saved up and bought an acetylene lamp which gave a super light but kept catching fire if you weren't careful with it! I was always glad when the cold winter evenings were over and the daylight longer.

I used to delight in seeing a waggon completed, but it seemed to take a long time. When the blacksmith had to 'shuck' the red-hot iron tyres onto the wooden wheel it was my job to go round pouring water on it, to stop the wheel from catching alight. Finally, the waggon had to be painted - red wheels and blue body, with genuine red lead paint for lasting. Then the farmer's name was painted on the front in bold letters. I well remember the chap who used to come to do this, he was a good signwriter, and would always do the best signs when he was three parts drunk! I suppose this was due to the fact that he did so many local inn signs, where he was well 'lushed' up with beer. I often wonder he didn't fall off the plank which he had rigged up to stand on!

Photo—J. S. Heward.

Stedham Mill

RIGHT ›

Editor's note: We believe that the cottage with the tall chimney is where Cecil was born, although in his sketch he shows it with a chimney stack at both ends.

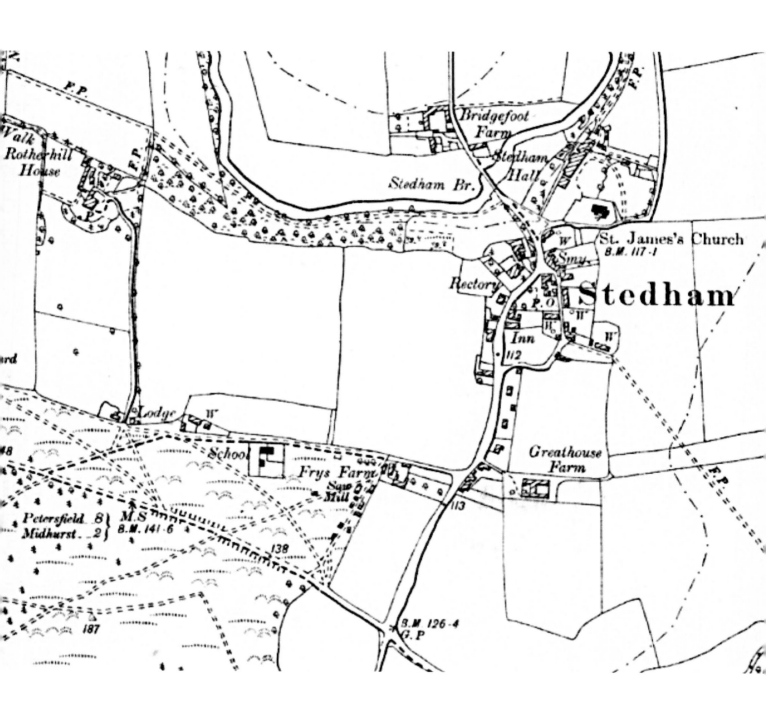

ABOVE: Stedham 1898

CHAPTER 1

THE VILLAGE OF STEDHAM FROM ABOUT 1907

To many people living in this village at the present time, it would most likely surprise them if they knew how very few houses there were here in the early 1900s, and seeing names on the old tombstones in the churchyard, it gives one some idea of families who **have long since died out, leaving no descendants in or around the village, names such as Andrews, Hammond and Ayling, etc.**

I remember that from the main road or Cross Roads as we knew it then, right down to the Collins Club, when it was just a field, on that side of the road and where the first house and the adjoining one stands, that is on the left hand side,

Christmas Row

just before one turns to go along to the School Lane, there used to be an orchard in this field where boys and sometimes girls, would slip through the hedge, to do a little apple 'scrumping'. But it was look out if the farmer caught you! One thing in the children's favour he was rather stout and couldn't run very fast, but should the local policeman catch you, one would feel his belt round ones backside, which wasn't a very pleasant experience.

On the right side of the road coming down from the Cross Road was the Farmhouse, which is now made into two houses. The front of the Farmhouse and around the sides are covered with rounded weather tiles, giving it a rather elaborate appearance compared with other cottages in the village. Mr. Eames was the name of the first farmer who lived there, followed by a Mr. Hills (Daddy Hills) as we knew him, and I can still remember some of the schoolgirls saying to us boys who were about to enter the orchard, 'Mind Daddy Hills don't catch you'.

Still on the right hand side of the road when entering the village there is a pair of

'Mind Daddy Hills don't catch you.'

old farm cottages, the second one is where we once lived after we were married and where our second son was born. It had a very long garden reaching down to a field and there were masses of raspberry canes when we went there at the bottom of the garden, so my wife was kept busy making raspberry jam. Also the toilet was a long way down the garden.

Next along from the two farm cottages was a little cottage where a Miss Hammond lived, a little old lady, a spinster. She used to peep round the side of her front window curtains and watch the children coming down School Lane home from school and if she saw anything amiss, she would most certainly inform the parents. She saw my wife once when she was on her way home from school playing marbles with the boys and she told my wife's mother that 'it was a most unladylike thing for a girl to do, to play marbles with the boys'. As you can imagine the girls used to call her an old so and so. Incidentally this little cottage where this old lady once lived is named Quince Cottage now. I don't think it had a name when we were going to school, only 'Old Mother Hammonds' cottage.

So proceeding down the right hand side of the village road, we come to another two semi detached houses. The first pair is where the West family lived, of whom I have written in my book entitled 'Stedham Families', the other semi detached pair was occupied by families named Christmas and Wakeford. And so on the right still and just on the corner is Gilbert's Workshop, that is where my father and uncles carried on their business of Builders, Decorators, Carpenters and Undertakers - like a good many other little Sussex villages had their little builders near by. Heyshott had the Parrys and if I mentioned them all, I should be going away from my Stedham Narrative.

A little winding road on the corner is known as the Alley, why I do not know, it leads to the footpath across the fields; on the right is a field (which is now the Sports Ground, where my wife's father used to umpire Cricket matches, and on the left is a row of cottages named Lavender Row.

Lavender used to grow all along the front gardens, hence the name, I suppose.

Retracing our steps back a little way instead of going across the fields to the Midhurst Road, is the old Grocer's shop, which is now derelict, but still proudly displays the name of Wild Family Grocers.

ABOVE: The Collins Club
BELOW: Wildes Store

Bridgefoot, Stedham.

They were grocers, bakers, pork butchers, the date was 1862, and Mrs. Wild used to serve all the villagers. (Strange I can still remember the names of the occupants of Lavender Row when I was a boy. First there was Old Billy Lambert, who lived for years with his two daughters, the Misses Lamberts, then there were the Petts, the Christmas's and the Merrits.) Opposite the shop is the big house where Mr. Wild the shopkeeper lived and two little cottages adjoining. Most Sussex villages have their family grocers still, I believe. Although in the towns of this county there are now Supermarkets, it's still nice to go into a little grocers shop to be served and not have to wander around with a wire basket hanging on ones arm.

Side facing the old shop on the left of the road, is a terrace of three houses South View, rightly named as they face the south downs and get the sunshine, when there is any. That was the home of the Stevens, Christmas's and my eldest uncle, but now they have all passed on. The houses still stand with new occupants. On the left of the derelict shop is the recreation ground, now with a swing and seesaw for the children. The members of the sports club keep the grass mown like a lovely lawn where in the summertime people can laze in the sun, have a picnic and enjoy seeing the cottage flowers near by. Also the grocers cart shed, stables, and piggeries are no more and a nice modern house and garden stand in their place. But then the recreation ground used to be a little meadow where a horse or cow or two were turned out to graze, and no motor cars in or through the village in those

days. It always seems a pity that little old shop stands empty and finished, no-one seems to buy it, rumours were about once it was going to be sold and turned into a dwelling house, but nothing happens now.

And so to proceed a little further down the street. On the right is a row of six houses, terraced houses, and my home now is No. 5 and it has been so for a number of years. It was my wife's home when she was a child. It is a three storied house, the top room was her bedroom and then, later, it was our boys' bedroom. Her paintings of flowers still hang in frames on the walls and the furniture there is the same as it has been for years and years now. From the front bedroom window, I see the garden of my old home, where I lived as a young boy, it was a kitchen garden then with a small lawn and plenty of fruit trees. Father had a little greenhouse where he loved to sit and smoke in the sunshine. We had large sheds with a few chickens and a nice summerhouse, where my brother and I smoked our first cigarettes.

Father and mother had gone to a Chrysanthemum Show on Southsea Common, so after coming out of school my brother said I am going to the shop (that was Mr. Wild's the grocers - later on in life, my brother Bert married their eldest daughter) to get a packet of Copes Courts Cigarettes (5 in a packet) for a penny or twopence (I forget the correct price). He was keen on getting a photo of a footballer, which they had in every packet. When he came back I asked him what he was going to do with the cigarettes, so he replied,

Retracing our steps back a little way instead of going across the fields to the Midhurst Road, is the old Grocer's shop....

'Smoke them, we'll share them.' So I said, 'You smoke three and I'll smoke two'. He then said, 'I'm sitting in the summer house to smoke mine'. At the back of the summer house was a big apple tree which we used to climb, so I said, 'I'm climbing up the apple tree to smoke mine'. Which we did. He was puffing away and so was I, when all of a sudden I felt so giddy and sick with the result that I fell out of the apple tree onto the roof of the summer house (which was of corrugated iron), wallop! It made my brother jump and cough, and me, well I was terribly sick on the summer house roof. When our parents returned home mother asked me if I was all right because she said I was looking very pale. She continued, ' I think you both should have an early night, I think you are tired.' We thought it best not to say what actually happened, so we went to bed early. However, after a few years of smoking we both decided to give it up and smoking is now a thing of the past for me. My wife never liked to see me walking around with a cigarette in my mouth, and now I can understand how she felt about it.

Our old home has been altered quite a lot since we lived there. It is situated almost in the centre of the village, there is an old barn quite near the back gate, which now garages cars. Beside the side wall of the barn yard, there used to be a little old hovel where a man used to live. He repaired shoes for people. He was a hunchback and mother and father always felt sorry for him and we used to take him in a Sunday dinner. People used to call him 'Old Corpy' why I don't know. I remember his surname was Moseley.

There was a triangular green opposite the front of our house, where the wheelwright used to keep the waggons after they had been repaired. Then on the left of the old barn and yard was the wheelwrights workshop where waggons were repaired. There now stands two semi-detached houses on the site where the smithy used to be, a place where they were always very busy. There are still several very old houses in the lower part of the village, whose roofs were of thatch in my young days, but now they have been brought up-to-date and tiled.

The right hand road takes one to where the flour mill used to be, and the left hand fork road leads to Bridgefoot and to the lanes, and here are scattered farms and farmhouses. The lanes are very beautiful

during the springtime with primroses, celandine and dandelions. I mention dandelions because that is where we used to go to gather dandelion flowers to make our wine, happy days they were. We always had a good supply of flower wines to give visitors a glass when they called. I should have mentioned the church which we always attended on Sundays, St. James, where we were christened, confirmed and married from. I think there is a booklet all about its history in the church.

‹ LEFT: sketch by Cecil
BELOW: Yarborough Terrace (No. 5) in the Alley, where Cecil lived in later life

Gnu Inn 1940

CHAPTER 2

THE GENTRY

People who were employed in the gentleman's houses when I was young were usually well treated by their employers especially during the festive season of Christmas. Indoor servants would get money in tips, while outdoor servants, such as cowmen, carters and workmen employed on the estate would be given a good round of beef or Christmas Pudding and mince pies, and were often given a small gift for the workmen's wives, and as wages were small it was made up to them in many other ways, such as a load of fire wood or a hundredweight of coal, but I believe all that generosity is finished, now. I suppose mainly because wages are much higher nowadays. I know my father-in-law used to be a carter on the estate in the village, and when it was a pheasant and partridge shoot, they used to entertain quite a number of gentlemen who enjoyed this form of sport. He would have to be about early in the morning with his horse and van; to follow the shooters and collect the birds so by the time he had finished at the end of the day, and had unharnessed his horse and fed it he was late getting home for his tea; but they were given a brace of rabbits - I mean those people on the estate who helped with the shoot, such as the carter, beaters and loaders, as they were known by, so that was a great help for the following day's dinner.

I think on the whole the gentry were mostly generous. For example when I was coming home from school one day two horse riders passed me and they drew up at our village grocers shop. The gentleman dismounted and gave me his reins, and said 'Here, boy, will you hold my horse, please?' I said, 'Yes, sir'. (Half afraid the horse would eat me, but it didn't). So he gave his lady friend a box of chocolates and turned to me and said, 'Here, boy, buy yourself some sweets.' And it was a half a crown, which he gave me. I did no more than run home to show mother what I had got. She said to me, 'Goodness, where on earth did you get that?' Of course, that was certainly a lot of money for a boy like me whose father would sometimes give me a penny if I went to the shop and bought a packet of Players cigarettes for him, and they used to be fourpence halfpenny for ten, and more often he would give me 5d and tell me to keep the halfpenny. Sometimes he would ask my brother to go and he would get the halfpenny. But mother was so surprised to see me with a half a crown and said to father, 'What do you think C. brought home. Sir Archie gave him half a crown for holding his horse.' And now to think they are out of circulation. My father always used to give my wife and myself and her brother and his wife half a crown for a Christmas present. Wish I'd saved mine, but I was hard up one day and had to spend it, never mind that was the way of life during those days.

The Timber Yard In 2021

F. Lintott

CHAPTER 3

THE TIMBER YARD

Run by Stedham men for a very long time, as far as I can remember back. Cover and Faulkner were the 'starters' and then Lintott Brothers took over; and one could see their timber carriage drawn by two heavy horses pulling a long load of trees, ready to be cut up by hand, and what hard work it was.

I remember seeing old Bridger spit on his hands before he started using the long Crosscut saw. There were at one time two covered pits, the tree would lay on the long side, and one man in the pit would pull the saw down, the other chap on top would pull the saw up. What a difference now with everything electrical and mechanical. Well enough they would wipe the sweat from their brows. Their wages were small in comparison with the work they did. They would cut oak and elm coffin boards and other boards to enable their fellow workmen to make all sorts of things in wood, portable sheds, etc., etc., of which I have one, £25 and it is still going strong 25 years later. All sections bolted together. They also made summer houses, goat sheds, bird tables, etc. How we loved to climb over the piles of trees, sometimes slipping as boys do, scraping or grazing our legs and shins, even the girls tried it. Then pushing our old pram to the timber yard to get a load of logs, pile it up, Mr. Lintott would say, three shillings a load. What about that now! How we loved that job and just before we started ageing my wife would come with me too, to help me push the pram with a super load home. Happy days, those.

Now the Lintotts are getting old, but there is still a partner left. Billy, older than I by three or four years, and still works making trug baskets. I bought one from him for £1. Not workman, every one of them a craftsman and make no mistake about it.

Pity there weren't more of them left, they lived and loved their work - if everyone did that now, it would be a different world to live in.

Stepping Stones. Stedham Mill

Stedham Mill

CHAPTER 4

THE OLD FLOUR MILL

Well known to us in 1908-09-10, when we were children, for in the early morning before we went to school it was always the children's job to go to fetch the separated milk from the Miller's dairy, where the cowman was busy separating, and what with the noise of the mill grinding corn and the separator going, it was a job to hear anybody speak.

Old Bob would shout 'Hurry up, you kids, let's have your cans'. And he would fill them up, topped with froth, all for a halfpenny. As we reached the miller's back entrance we would stand and stare at the covered waggon arriving loaded up with corn, ready to be taken to the top loft and from thence it was wheeled across a covered 'walk over' to the mill. Two men on the go all the time, with a sack of corn in their wheelbarrow. Nearby were the flood gates, in those days operated by hand and so regulated, the water would rush through to set the mill wheels operating and so the round stones would start revolving, and in between them the corn would be turned into flour. When it was time for the men to go home their clothes and head gear would be white with flour as if they had been out in a snowstorm.

Of course, we could not stand staring at the men for long, otherwise we would have been late for school. Often, mother would say 'Come on, you've been a long time this morning. Now hurry up off to school, otherwise you'll be late. So off we went. We always managed to stay down at the mill a little longer during school holidays.

The water now rushes over the weir, but four of the stepping stones are missing, so one has to cross over the narrow concrete bridge to get to the lanes up Mill Anger. [The Hangar?]

Stedham Mill as remembered by Cecil

forward to fishing, cricket and all sorts of games, interests and excitements, climbing the downs, racing, football, etc., etc. And so as age progresses, young lads and lasses tend to pay a little attention to each other and many eventually fall in love. Sometimes it's only temporary infatuation, and sometimes it's forever (mine was the latter) and then it's good to have each others company. Sometimes they become engaged, oh, so happy, and then the thrill of talking about getting married and so come the wedding bells.

How I enjoy writing about all this, and now what comes next – a family maybe? Then finally, old age creeps on. If you are healthy, it's not so bad, and what do you do if you are still in love for many years, you fuse your lives together, helping each other, playing cards together. Then, one sad day, it's goodbye. One is left to manage on one's own, a difficult job sometimes, maybe. Just left with happy memories and looking forward to meeting your loved one again in the Happy Land; without this thought, how awful the last part of life would be.

Children in those days always seemed to enjoy their games and pastimes, such as marbles, hoops and tops, etc., these I will tell you about later. As one gets older so one's fingers and hands ache from writing, so now I must rest a while, before proceeding with my story - if one can call it such.

BELOW: Stedham School 1986 | PHOTO: courtesy of Reg Symonds

Grandad would turn
his half a dozen cows
out on the common
and it was our job
to watch them to see
they didn't stray.

CHAPTER 8

SCHOOL HOLIDAYS

Everyone, needless to say, was very happy when the school closed down for five weeks summer holidays.

Some children went with their mothers hop-picking. My wife did and she has told me how very hungry they got, always had a ravenous appetite, due I suppose to the smell of the hops. My brother and myself used to love to go to our grandfather's small-holding, which was about a mile and a half away from our home village and was just a small hamlet surrounded by common and heath land.

Grandad would turn his half a dozen cows out on the common and it was our job to watch them to see they didn't stray. In their farm house was a large bread oven, where my uncle and aunt baked bread, rolls and cakes and then uncle would deliver them with his horse and cart. It was on Saturday mornings the rolls were made and us boys had to mark them with a special knife, three marks on the top, they were delicious when they came out of the oven all nice and hot.

Come mangel hoeing time, grandfather would say to us, 'Ah, it won't be long now afore Mass Driver arrives'. And he was often right to the day, for old Driver was his name and he was, we always thought, a fairly respectable tramp. He used to sleep in a hovel where grandfather kept hay and straw for the cows. He wore corduroy trousers, yoked up with straps just below his knees, his jacket was of heavy brown tweed. He used to go to Grandfather's house and Grandmother would give him a screw of tea and some milk in his billycan. He usually bought bread and cheese from them, and a piece of fat pork, which he seemed to enjoy for his midday meal. Alternatively, it would be bread and cheese and an onion (he carried several of these in his pockets). He would always wash in the stream which ran along the bottom of the meadow, we used to sit and talk to him while he was having his midday meal, and ask him where he came from, was he married, did he have any sons or daughters. He used to smile and say well, if you ask questions that is the way you learn. But it didn't matter how many questions you asked him, he would never divulge where he came from or where he went to, in fact he was most evasive. Grandfather was always very satisfied with the way he worked, while grandmother would say, 'That man's a mystery. There's no doubt about it!' Most evenings he would watch us play cricket, for there was quite a lot of short grass outside Grandfather's farm house. It was almost like a lawn, due to the fact that there were many rabbits about. They used to nibble the grass, especially during dry summers. Also there used to be quite a few little red squirrels about in those days, but one hardly sees them now in this part of Sussex, but there are quite a number of grey squirrels which are really tree rats.

My grandfather used to employ a lad. His name, I remember, was Charlie Bacon. He used to do quite a number of jobs on the farm. He would have days off now and again. Once, father bought some laying hens from Grandfather and it was Charlie's job to put these half a dozen hens into a sack to take to my father's chicken run. As he was on his way to our house it was getting late and he put the sack down to have a rest, and the silly fellow didn't tie up the mouth of the sack, as a result the chickens all flew out and roosted up a fir tree. It was almost dark by then, so next morning early, Charlie had to retrace his steps and climb up the tree to get the hens down. It took him a long time as he had to carry the sack with him to put the hens in and what a job that was! Grandfather was cross with him and said, 'Lor-Massy O, where's your sense.'

Then one day when Charlie had gone home for a couple of days, he wanted someone to take Dolly, the Jersey cow, to a neighbouring farm to have her mated with this farmer's bull. As I was fond of this little Jersey he said to me, 'Now you're a bit older, Boy, you could take her, couldn't you?' I said, ' 'course I can, Grandad.' And so it was arranged. He put a halter on the cow and off we went. 'Now don't be in a hurry, Lad,' he said, and so I returned with the cow. She most certainly didn't approve of the bull's advances, so home we had to come. Grandfather's first words to me were, 'Well did she stand, Laddie,' and I said, 'No, Grandad, she kept moving round and round.' He said, 'Dang her ole head, you'll have to take her over there again in a month's time.' And so life went on.

The routine was much the same week after week on the little small-holding. My father regularly paid his parents a visit every Tuesday evening, whether it was light or dark, wet or fine, he very rarely missed, and so brother and I wanted to go too. When it became almost dark on the bank by the side of the road, numerous glow worms were showing off their phosphorescent light, and the nightjar was making jarring noises in the fir trees not too far distant. I don't know why but I have not heard it for years since, and one wonders if they have become extinct. During the day the footpaths were edged by gorse bushes, where not many years ago now I used to go and pick the blossoms to make a delicious wine. Also linnets, yellow hammers and long tailed tits would nest in the gorse bushes. Often one could hear the squeal of a rabbit mesmerised by a stoat or a weasel and one always felt sorry for the poor rabbit. Sometimes in the early morning one would see a deer dart away in the green of the birch trees.

My father used to buy antique furniture and repair it where necessary, then resell it. This was to supplement his small income and ours was quite a large house and old, and often needed repairs. However, we were a very happy family, and since the house has been sold now other tenants have said there always seemed to be a happy atmosphere surrounding the place. Sometimes father could pick up a good piece of antique furniture. I remember once he bought a Queen Anne claw and ball foot table. A local Doctor saw it and offered father £50 for it, at the time father accepted his offer and we heard later that this Doctor sold it to someone in America for £100. Father, as you can imagine, was a little more than cross to hear this news.

My mother, like other women, used to make a little wine and it was always rhubarb, and the strange part of that wine was nobody would drink it, only me. With a result that she only made a gallon at a time, corked it up and placed it down the cellar.

We had an old-fashioned mangle standing in the corner of the kitchen and it was always my job to mangle the sheets, towels, tea towels, etc. I always thought I could do it better than anyone else, I didn't mind doing that job at all. The job I didn't like doing was cleaning the knives on the old knife board, it was always a job to clean them where the handle joined the steel blade of the knife.

However, it was either my job or my brother's, to get the wood and coal in. How well I remember when I was very small, only about six years old, it was washing day and mother was in the garden, hanging out the washing, when a large piece of wood fell out of the copper hole and was burning away on the brick floor of the kitchen. I didn't know at the time what to do, so I did no more than unbutton trousers and made water on it to put it out! Mother was so cross with me she took me into the living room and laid me across her knee and gave my bottom a good tanning, and said "that'll teach you." I never did it again, and for days I remember I felt the result of that spanking.

During our summer holidays, we usually had a Sunday School outing, which meant that we were taken by Charabanc to Bognor for the day and it used to be a bit of a headache for the Rector, who seemed to take charge both coming and going. He used to have a roll call when we started, one when we went to a restaurant for dinner and one when it was time to leave. Often there was a child or two missing, which meant someone had to start hunting for them. I remember we always used to sing on our way home, it was usually 'We've all been to Bognor and had a happy day'.

Then sometimes for a change, we would all go to the South Downs. Usually there would be about two or three dozen children waiting in good time outside of the Rectory, as that was the assembly point. Then two farm waggons would arrive, about 10 o'clock in the morning, the men who then set about getting forms from where the Sunday School was held and arranging them in the waggons. The waggons travelled one behind the other for about a mile and a half and one went one way and one the other, and it used to be great fun for the children to guess whose waggon was going to arrive first. We always seemed to go to the same spot every time we journeyed to the Downs. It was a pleasant valley where orchids grew and flowers that wouldn't be seen anywhere else, only on the Downs.

Well, on arrival one waggon always got there first and when the other one came along there was a loud cheer. After unloading, the grown-ups (some parents and some teachers) commenced getting all the food - cakes, sandwiches, etc., from boxes under the waggons. Of course, every child had to bring their own mug for their tea, and it wasn't long before all the hungry children were well fed. Prior to that we all had to sing grace. After tea the children were warned not to wander too far away and get lost and when the Rector blew a whistle loud, it was time to assemble to go home. I remember well seeing one boy roll down the Downs and he finished up winding himself when he collided with a tree. Now when the horses were shut in the traces, off we went. Most of the youngsters were tired and dirty, but nearly all the parents were there to meet them. The children all sang 'For He's a Jolly Good Fellow' to the Rector for looking after them, and no doubt there was a bath ready for them when they reached home.

Salisbury Cathedral

CHAPTER 9

WILTSHIRE

Some years father or mother would take us two boys, Bert and myself - that's my brother's name (he has passed away now) to Wiltshire for a week or fortnight during our summer holidays. We stayed with mother's eldest sister and her husband in a small thatched cottage at Thruxton, which was near a little village called Cholderton.

At the back of their house was a grassy hill, with a windmill. I suppose it was part of Wiltshire downland, we would amuse ourselves for hours, by seeing how many different types of butterflies there were on that hill, then trying to catch grasshoppers: It always pleased aunt if we took her a handful of wildflowers or spindleberries, which grew in profusion on that hill.

Uncle was a Head Keeper for the gentleman who lived in the big county house not far away from uncle's cottage and uncle's hobby was gardening. I can remember what lovely big onions he grew. There were two Under Keepers, Will Hackman, always a smiling sort of man, then the other keeper was Charlie Robinson, uncle nicknamed him Moses (why I do not know) perhaps it was because he was a little on the scruffy side. When there was a shoot on, and before the gentlemen shooters had assembled outside the Head Keeper's cottage, uncle held an inspection of the keepers under him, also the loaders and stoppers. It was almost like our army inspections and reminded me of such. They had to be correctly dressed with Keepers jackets. (A Keepers jacket had two wide side pockets either side opening from the inside of the jacket.) It was a pleasing sight for us two brothers to watch and we could watch at a distance, that was so we shouldn't get in anyone's way. Uncle wasn't beyond telling the under keepers to get their hair cut, if he thought it was necessary. Poor old Moses never appeared to be very happy when it was a big shoot day, they all had to have polished boots and leggings and carry their guns correctly under their arm.

There is no doubt uncle was a very strict man and even the two black retriever dogs had to be obedient and 'sit' until the guns moved off. (Their names were Nelson and Smoker, and beautiful dogs they were.) When the guns moved they had to follow to heel, if they were obedient they received a pat from uncle, if they weren't he shouted at them, which made them 'cowed down'. Their homes were kennels the other side of the road, near the trees. It all seemed very quiet after they had left, except for the banging of the guns near the spinney which was about a mile away, and as one went over the Newton Toney road to cross to the field which took one to the footpath to the spinney. Once when we were there, there was a mass of pale blue chicory growing in this field, being summer time. With a blue sky overhead and the pale blue across the whole field it was a beautiful sight which has remained in my memory ever since; it would have delighted an artist, no doubt.

We used to like to go through the spinney, it was like a long tunnel of overhanging

Their names were Nelson and Smoker, and beautiful dogs they were.

hazel nut trees, at the other end we came to the village of Cholderton. A pretty little village, with the church near the school where my cousins used to go when they were young. It had a little general shop, including a Post office, and newspapers sold there. Also there ran a little stream through the village with white painted rails either side, the little shop we used to go to to buy sweets if uncle gave us a little pocket money. The keeper's cottage was a lovely old fashioned place, with a lot of honeysuckle growing over the porch and uncle was very fond of growing phlox. There always seemed a lot of bees around, I remember. The house a little way up the lane was where the Bailiff lived, he kept bees and goats, and auntie used to get her goats milk from him. We used to enjoy a glass of that milk most mornings. Almost opposite uncle's house was a big brick building which was stables and a covered compound where the horses used to gallop around. We spent hours watching these lovely Arab horses with their foals. From the main entrance of the stables were some stone stairs to the rooms above where the grooms slept and lived. There always seemed to be something going on to interest us boys. Often we would go to the bottom of the lane, for on the left was the cart shed, where the waggons and some farm implements were kept, and we would play there when there was no one about, climbing on the waggons.

Shooting day was different, for the horses were brought there to get the light waggons to take the shooters lunch around and pick up the birds. How we enjoyed ourselves on those holidays, and always wanted to go again. I remember we were met at Grately station with a dog cart driven by an uncle of ours (not the keeper), and he drove us there again when it was time to go home. How we enjoyed auntie's cooking, especially rabbit pie. We were always hungry. Then ofttimes we would go down to the bottom of the lane and sit on the gate and watch the soldiers go by on their horses, drawing their guns and limbers, and didn't they kick up a dust in the hot summertime, going down the Andover Road from Salisbury Plain and on through to Larkhill. They used to post a squad of infantrymen to direct the others which way to go and they squatted around by the gate at the bottom of our lane. They would give us their waterbottles to take to the cottage to fill them as the dust made them thirsty. If there were not too many of them aunt would send them some tea in her milk cans. We used to enjoy every minute of our holiday with Aunt Evie and Uncle Alf.

Every Wednesday the baker would call on aunt, and she had to take bread and buns, sometimes cakes for the week. He also had to make a call at the other cottages nearby and to the stable boys in their quarters. The baker's shop was at Shipton, several miles away. Aunt would always make the baker a cup of tea, and while that was

brewing he would come out and have a game of cricket with us boys. He would spend about half an hour with us and the other customers before returning home to Shipton. In those days Shipton was a typical Wiltshire village with the usual little shop or two; but maybe it has grown since that far off time. He was a young man with a wonderful sense of humour, his name was Charlie Cheeseman. On our holiday I remember my suit had begun to get a bit tatty and untidy, due to the fact that I climbed too many trees, so auntie and I walked to Shipton, while my brother went with uncle to try and find some pheasants eggs to put under a hen to hatch out. While in Shipton, my aunt took me into a little drapers and out-fitters shop and bought me a new grey tweed suit, and when I wore it I felt like little Lord Fauntleroy! It was a Norfolk jacket style with a belt round the waist, with matching knee breeches. I remember it was a long walk to Shipton village and back. There were no buses or motors in those days and the roads were rough and chalky, so both aunt and I were tired when we got back to her cottage. However, you can imagine how proud I was of my new suit when we returned home after a lovely holiday in Wiltshire.

CHAPTER 10

PORTSMOUTH

Sometimes Father would like to give us a pleasant surprise during our Summer holidays, so one evening he said "I want you boys to be in bed in good time tonight as I'm taking you out for the day tomorrow which means rising early for we shall be going by train".

He had previously arranged with the driver of the milk cart who takes the early morning milk to the station to give us a lift and we would be waiting by our front gate at 6.15 am, the time he came along, and by so doing we were able to get to our destination (which was Portsmouth) nice and early by catching the down train from Petersfield. We were so excited we had difficulty in eating our breakfast. Father had a programme all mapped out for us. First we would go along to South Parade Pier and from there we could see the ships of the Royal Navy leaving or going to the harbour. Once we saw a huge liner heading for the Docks.

After spending quite a time there he would take us to Canoe Lake to sail our yachts. We enjoyed doing this but one had to place the yacht windward to get to the other side and so we would race round the lake hoping to get there before the boat. Father

got tired of watching us and dropped off to sleep on the seat. At last he awoke and said it was nearly lunch time and so we returned to South Parade Pier. From there we went by tramcar to the Sailors Rest Restaurant in Commercial Road and like most boys we were always hungry and ready for a meal. Afterwards we went to Clarence Pier and to the Fun Fair. That was too noisy for Father and it was not long before we had to walk to the station and so on the train home. The milk cart was waiting for us at the end of the journey and Mother was pleased to see us home again safe and sound. After asking Father if he gave the driver of the cart a sixpenny tip, which we noticed he did, we always went to the farm where he worked each day to get our daily milk, taking our milk can. The cowman always gave us good measure. We used to like to stand and watch the milk trickling down the cooler, and thence into the churns. He would always help us up to the steps of the dairy when it was frosty and if they were slippery. Father always gave him a cigar at Christmas for his kindness.

Girl with Hoop by Renoir

CHAPTER 11

GAMES, PASTIMES, DANCES

Our games were regulated according to the time of the year; of course, there were always the usual ones, cricket and football. Cricket, of course, played during the summer. In between seasons we played Follow-on Marbles on the way to school and the same coming home.

Sometimes we had a ring of marbles in the playground which the girls would like to watch from the fence at the top of the playground. Separating the girls' playground from the boys was a stone and brick wall, with broken glass set on the top in cement or mortar, which I always thought was a cruel idea on somebody's part. However, let's get back to the question of games. Hoops were always popular. Girls would have a hoop made at the local timber yard, where they used to make similar hoops for barrels. They used to be as good as bicycles to boys and girls in those days, girls would tail their wooden hoops with a stick and boys would have an iron hoop which the blacksmith would make for sixpence. They had a strong wire bent over at the end, which would act as a brake (called Skidders) for the hoop. Boys and girls had hoop races and of course there were

no cars or lorries to hinder their progress - just sometimes a pony or cart or a farm waggon, and that wasn't very often. Whips and tops were often played by both girls and boys, mainly by boys though. There were two types of wooden tops, the stumpy one which had painted rings around it. Then there was the mushroom top. Both had a little piece of steel or lead inserted at the base; the method of starting these tops was as follows, first you had a string tied to the top of a stick, making the whip. You bound the string round the top where the coloured rings were, placed the top under your left heel, held the top where the string was tied and gave it a sharp pull at the same time releasing the top from your heel. This gives the top a spinning start and from then on you whip it to keep it revolving. Incidentally, the mushroom types were the hardest to start, especially if it wasn't held straight under your heel - then it would just wobble away sideways. We were not allowed out of the playground during playtime, so we had to amuse ourselves in our respective playgrounds. Girls were not supposed to come into the boys' playground and vice versa, but sometimes the rules were broken!

As time passed and winter evenings came upon us, so the pattern of life altered. Instead of outdoor games and sport as in the summer, we were confined to indoor pursuits when the evenings were long and dark. A good many of the working population of our small village would have probably sat around a nice fire, perhaps talking of the day's happenings, sometimes reading or playing cards. We played various games in the winter evenings such as Ludo, Draughts, Snakes and Ladders, and then card games, Donkey, Beat your Neighbour Out of Doors, Rummy and Snap just to mention a few. Then we had a game with rings, one had six rings to throw on a board which had hooks to each number, the highest number was twenty, which was in the middle of the board and one had to see who could score most numbers. In latter

some fir cones or pinies or wood to start it again. When eight-thirty came Father would say, 'Come on you boys, it's time you went to bed. Pack up your games and see about it.' And so, after a drink of milk and a biscuit, away we went. It wasn't long after we said our prayers we were in bed and asleep. My brother used to dream a lot, and have many nightmares, which woke me up. Someone seemed to be after him all the time in his dreams, so I was jolly glad when he went off to sleep again.

Old rifle range / dance hall / function room

years my wife and myself preferred our two card games which were cribbage and rummy.

Father would always like to keep poking the fire to make it burn brighter and mother was often heard to say, 'For goodness sake, Will, leave the fire alone or else you'll poke it out.' Sometimes this did happen and he would have to go to the woodhouse with his candle-lantern to get

Mother belonged to the Women's Institute and they held their meetings in the Memorial Hall in the village. This took place in the afternoons, but sometimes of an evening she would go to a Whist Drive. Sometimes she won a prize, usually the Booby or nothing at all. Father used to like her to go as it made a change for her. As my brother and I got older we joined the village club and sat and watched men play Billiards and Cork Pools and sometimes shove-halfpenny. Of course, as time went on we joined in these games as well, but soon we wanted to do something different. My brother formed a Concert Party with lads of the village, they spent a lot of time practising and singing, plays and comedy mostly. They bought a little harmonium and had quite an orchestra! They named the Concert Party 'Herbert's Erbs', because Bert's full name was Herbert. He was dead keen on making this party a success, he studied conjuring and eventually became a member of the Magic Circle and would travel round outlying villages giving shows in aid of charity. They all enjoyed it and girls joined the party as well. There was singing and dancing on the programmes. They usually took enough money to pay for a little refreshment by the way of drinks after the show, this was not my way of enjoying myself, but sometimes they would ask me to take the money at the door, which I did. One of their pals would show people to their seats, he always wore evening dress, but I couldn't be bothered to do that.

I was always very keen on shooting, so a Miniature Rifle Club was formed in the village which I joined and we had a Rifle Range built. This was fifty yards long and our shooting range was 25 feet. We had winding wheels and wires to wind the targets in position for shooting and so we could wind them back to see the results. We paid 3d for seven shots, so it usually cost each one of us a shilling for an evening's shooting. The Club was opened once a month and we used to shoot against other villages that had a range. Each month a local gentleman gave a silver spoon for the best shot in three months. I was very proud to win it once and still have it. I was shooting against a very experienced chap, a local gardener, he had a handicap which helped me shoot against him. He was very annoyed by me winning, as he had already won five spoons and wanted one more to make his half dozen, but he was unlucky and very amazed to think, as he put it, beaten by a slip of a boy like that! My father was pleased to think I won and had my initials engraved on the spoon handle, but now after years of my wife proudly cleaning it, my initials are almost worn off. I think I took after my father, he was keen on shooting and also joined the club. We often used to go to the Fir plantation and wait for pigeons to come in to roost - they provided us with many a pigeon pie. Although there is not much on a pigeon only the breast, so one had to shoot several to get a good meal.

As we grew up our ways of life changed. I have already said my brother was keen on entertainments, conjuring, and as he got older his hobby was photography and cameras. Whilst I was keen on going to dances and riding a motorbike, and sometimes falling off it! I always think my brother's hobby was very worthwhile, nevertheless expensive, and mine was too. I used to think petrol was expensive at one time, at three shillings a gallon; but, oh dear, look at the price of it now!

> **He was dead keen on making this party a success, he studied conjuring and eventually became a member of the Magic Circle....**

The dances I used to enjoy were known in our village as 'sixpenny hops' and they took place in the rifle range, which I have already spoken about. Everyone had to dance on hard, compressed soil, as the first part of the Rifle Range was where we laid our mats down to do our shooting. A portable table was opened up in the space at the back, whereupon the refreshments were laid out in the dancing interval for dancers to come and have coffee or teacakes etc; this was organised by the ladies, who were keen to make it a pleasant evening. Of course, some of the ladies didn't dance, but used to sit and look on, and often one could hear a remark from them, especially if you were dancing near where they were sitting. 'Good gracious, look at that couple!'

You must remember as one progressed down the length of the building it was a case of dancing almost in darkness, with the exception of perhaps half a dozen candle lanterns dotted here and there. It was, of course, illuminated at the bottom of the building, where the targets were situated on their wire railways, and I might mention here and now, it was some time before some couples reached the target area, or should I say, the illuminated area, owing to the fact that quite a lot of kissing and cuddling took place in the dark area! However, I well remember it was all good fun and incidentally, during the last waltz, which I remember was nearly always 'Good night, Sweetheart, all dreams are for you', was always an extremely slow one.

Our band was composed of a piano, two violins, a cello, and sometimes a melodeon or else an harmonica. The gardener from the big house was always a good sport. Mr. Chapman was his name, and he loved to join in, but he was also the M. C., and when it came to the Lancers he would always say, 'Now gentlemen, no taking the ladies off their feet'. But us lads noticed when he joined in he was the first one to disobey the rule, in fact you could see a sly smile on his face, when he was watching and this happened often. Then he would say, smiling, 'Now then boys, now then boys'.

Besides being a good sport as M.C. he was an excellent head gardener at the house called 'Rotherhill'. You reached it by going up School lane. My dear wife used to be the parlourmaid there and we spent many happy courting times while she was there. She has remarked to me often it was a pleasure to work for the Wills family. The old gentleman was a retired doctor, and when we became engaged his son was coming down the drive in his old car on his way to see his girl and they had just become engaged as well, so he stopped the car and said to me, 'Congratulations, old chap. We are both in the same boat now.' and as he drove off one of the legs of his pyjamas was sticking out of his case, so I presumed he packed in a hurry. Now he has passed on, his wife married again and lost her second husband but they have two sons, one always likes to see me and have a chat, and the subject is usually his father. Still, all that is past, the old rifle range was demolished and a village hall built in its place, where they hold Parish Council meetings, Women's Institute members meet there, and it's also let for

... owing to the fact that quite a lot of kissing and cuddling took place in the dark area!

Herbert's 'Erbs

Wedding reception, etc., etc., but no old time dancing, in fact it's not really as long as the old Rifle Range!

One last word about the dances, I ought to have mentioned that after dancing with a lady, it was always considered good manners to escort her back to her seat, and if you knew her, kiss her gently on her cheek and she would most likely say thank you for the dance. You would probably say now, how terribly romantic, well to most young people in my youthful days I suppose it was, when you sometimes would dance with your partner cheek to cheek; however, like fashion and seasons, dances change over the years. Personally, I cannot see anything connected with romance in present day dances. Never mind the youth seem to enjoy themselves with their Discos, nevertheless.

Our village club is situated near the Memorial Hall, for that is now the building which replaced the old Rifle Range, but the village club has certainly altered a lot since I joined at the age of 15. This club was founded by a Church of England clergyman, by the name of Collins and it is now named the Collins Club. Previous to that it was called the Coffee Tavern, that was because one could buy coffee or cocoa in preference to intoxicating drinks. There was only one room and that housed the billiard table, and the older men would sit around the fire and talk. Alternatively, they would sit at the table and play card games such as cribbage, etc. Also, there was a shove-halfpenny board on one of the tables, which used to be very popular with some of the men. In fact, father-in-law was a very good player, and I remember it was always a job to beat him. There used to be a rule that when a game of billiards or snooker was taking place, whistling or making an unnecessary noise was not allowed and there was no doubt that rule was most strictly adhered to. There was a top room over the Club room where meetings of all descriptions were held, committee meetings, Band of Hope, Sunday School Treats, and on Sunday afternoons, the Wesleyan Methodists used to hold a service there and often it was packed with people.

Now the top room has been turned into a flat for the Caretaker and his wife to live in. There used to be a good library of books housed there and a Roll of Honour was beautifully inscribed, hung over the fireplace, with names of the men who served and were wounded, and some killed in the first World War. The names of those who were killed were printed in gold, those who served overseas in red, and those who served at home in Great Britain in blue. My name was in red. I went into the top room some long time ago, and they were clearing out. The Roll of Honour laid screwed up on the floor, and now they say, 'We will remember them' - sometimes I have my doubts. I remember that after the first World War, there was a lot of unemployment, but of course not on such a large scale as today, due I suppose, to the fact that there are more people about.

The Stedham Yew which
hasn't changed for 1,000 years
(possibly 2,500 years).
PHOTO: Dawn Cansfield

CHAPTER 12

CHANGES

Our little village is no longer a little village. Council houses have sprung up over the twenty acre field, and that field used to grow a lovely crop of corn, interspersed with poppies, and now new roads are leading to the houses, and people coming and going in their cars, instead of the peace and quiet as it used to be in our younger days.

Now a word about Mill Lane, as you walk past the church and the Manor House, past the drive, Mill Lane starts there. It used to be a rough road, made rough, no doubt, by the Miller's covered waggon. This was drawn by two heavy Shire horses and was always well looked after. They would go about three miles away to the nearest town station and collect the sacks of wheat and take them to the mill to be ground into flour. We used to love to stand at the Mill door and watch the machines go round and round, grinding the wheat into flour. It was a busy time then for the miller and his men, and we were told not to get in their way. So then we went round to the side door of the miller's house to collect our skimmed milk, and watch the men separating it. Each child handed in

their milk cans and went home with them filled up for halfpenny a can full. Going up the hill as we left the mill we used to dip our fingers into the top froth and make believe it was ice cream.

Our mothers used to make big rice puddings with it, and if there wasn't a fire lit in the range, she would send us to the Bakehouse with the pudding to ask the baker to put it in the oven when the bread comes out. To do this we were charged one penny, and of course at Christmas time some of the villagers asked to put their birds in the bread oven, that is if they only had a small oven in their grates. The Baker was a very old man and like other old men in the village would walk around with his bootlaces undone. Maybe it was because they were too much trouble for them to lace up properly, it was a wonder sometimes they didn't trip up. The baker's name was Bob Martin, he had no children and he and his wife lived in a little thatched cottage almost opposite the little drapers shop. This shop was much smaller than the grocers, but even now, that is turned into a grocery and greengrocer store.

The grocers shop is now derelict, but in the early years it was a very thriving business, open early in the morning, closing late at night, 10 o'clock. It always had a good selection of biscuits, which were in tins, and sacks of dried peas, rice, porage oats and sugar, weighed on the scales and sold according to weight.

The house where the grocer lived was opposite the shop, an imposing building with rounded chimneys, and the front of the buildings bears the date 1862. The grocer used to keep pigs behind where the cart sheds stood, which was adjoining his garden. This was near the footpath past the row of houses known as Lavender Row, and Wednesday when the shop was closed for half a day, was pig killing time, for he always sold his own pork and would keep sides of bacon up his chimney to cure for rashers. My mother would always place an order there each week for liver and crow and about once every three weeks would buy a piece of pork for roasting. It always tasted delicious, as the pigs were fed on the surplus bread which remained unsold, mixed with water, mashed potatoes and barley meal. The boys of the village would ask for the pig's bladder, to blow up and play football with. Another part of the pig mother would buy was the scraps of fat, which were sold cheap and were bought by women of the village to make scrap pies of, which made with currants, etc. was like the Christmas Mince Pie and very nice it was too.

The grocers had a two wheeled bread van, horse drawn, which one of his men by the name of Frank Underwood would drive around outlying villages delivering the loaves of bread, buns and cakes. Also they had a hand cart which they used to deliver the bread round the village. It used to take Mr. Underwood a long time to finish his deliveries and longer still in the winter time when it was dark, as they only had two candle lamps on the cart, one either side, and when it came to cleaning out the stable, putting the cart and horse away, it had to be done with either a candle lantern or a paraffin oil storm lantern, as there was no electric light or gas in the village in those days. I still have my Grandfather's old carriage lamp fixed up outside of my front door with an electric candle light inside. I have thought how Grandfather would have appreciated a light as such on his cart, or even in their little farm cottage. But it was surprising how folks got accustomed to the oil lamp or candlelight, and so not being used to the bright light of electricity, one could see to walk about in the dark much easier than people could now-a-days.

OUR
VERY FIRST HAPPY
MARRIED SNAPS we went to

Weston-super-mare, on a London too Bath Sunday,
Excursion, first stop Slough, where we started from.
fortunately we had our Macs & an umbrella.

Dec 4th 1926.

A stormy day
Weston-super-mare 1927

Weston super-mare

Weston-super-mare

CHAPTER 13

FAMILY LIFE

Now a word or two about family life. We as a family were always very happy together, we had no television or radio to start with, but we used to amuse ourselves playing games, reading comics or books which were given to us as presents, or we may have won a book at school as a prize for lessons well done. As time passed on, wireless became the accepted thing, and that started as a Crystal set.

As far as I can remember Crystal sets were started round about the year 1924 to 1925. Before we were married or even engaged my fiancee was employed in gentleman's service in Haslemere, but after three years of courtship we then became engaged. While she was working at Haslemere I made her a little Crystal set, which of course everyone considered was a wonderful invention in those days. I had to get permission from her employers who were Sir Algernon and Lady Methuen, before I could erect an aerial from a tree in the drive to a chimney above the servants hall, however that was granted and before

long everyone was trying to see who could find the sensitive spot on the crystal, and one had to wear headphones which were attached to the set, and it was always a tricky job to get 2LO the London Radio station, but it was surprising how clear the reception was.

After the Crystal set, one, two and three valve sets came on the market, with a loud speaker attached with a lead from the set, which was from the start a horn type speaker, usually made by a firm named Amplion, and one could take a magazine called 'Amateur Radio' and there was another one 'Popular Radio' and these magazines gave plans and diagrams showing how one could make their own wireless set. And then quite a number of firms in due course, incorporated a loud speaker enclosed in nicely polished wood cabinets, and then came radiograms, which were quite a piece of furniture and very expensive. Every spare moment I used to study radio and so in the early part of my married life I obtained employment with a radio firm, Kolster Brandes Ltd., of Slough, then the business was transferred to Sidcup, Kent and so I moved there with them, and we bought our first house there. We were so happy there, it was a lovely little semi-detached new style bungalow with two bedrooms upstairs, kitchenette, dining and drawing room and a small room from the hall which we named the Den, (why I don't know). What pleased us both was the nice big garden, we were very keen

gardeners, my wife did the flowers, me the vegetables. She was a good gardener, maybe it could have been inherited, as her father was a gardener, and also she loved reading garden books, buying her seeds, etc. I used to do the heavy spade work for her. I think her favourite flowers were pinks and pansies, but I know she loved them all. At the bottom of the garden it was completely wild, with masses of bluebells growing there, and we left it like that because it was so nice and peaceful and we used to relax there in our deck chairs. It reminds me of a little quotation which is framed in our bedroom, above the mantlepiece, which my wife put there a long time ago, with a birthday card to me. It had a lovely coloured picture of pansies and which reads:

> *The kiss of the sun for pardon*
> *The song of the birds for birth*
> *One is nearer God's heart in a garden*
> *Than anywhere else on earth.*

There were Canterbury bells growing outside of the kitchen, under the window, and in the front border mauve and yellow violas. We had to work very hard to get our garden into good shape and be able to grow the vegetables, as previously the whole estate was a wood. Everyone used to help each other to remove the massive tree stumps which were sticking up from the ground level quite two feet, and so on Sunday it was good fun, especially after digging all round a stump it would start to wobble, so with a united effort of our neighbours, we eventually cleared our garden plots. We were all young and strong then. Now after 55 years of happy married life I stroll all alone in my garden thinking of my dear one and looking forward to being with her again in that Heavenly Garden.

LEFT: William, Ada and Eddie
BELOW: William, Ada and Bert

ABOUT THE MIDHURST SOCIETY

For everyone who cares about the heritage of Midhurst and the surrounding villages

The Society was formed in 1960 to stimulate public interest in Midhurst and the surrounding villages, promote high standards of planning and architecture, encourage the preservation, development and improvement of local features of historic and community interest, and engage with the public through meetings, lectures, exhibitions and publications.

The Society is as relevant today as it was half a century ago and by promoting preservation, an active heritage group can make a real difference. We have distilled our aims as follows: making Midhurst a better place to live, work and enjoy.

The Midhurst heritage

Midhurst is a unique historic town set at the heart of the South Downs National Park. It is surrounded by beautiful villages and magnificent countryside. Its remarkable history is represented in a range of outstanding buildings spanning many centuries, together with the atmospheric Cowdray Ruins closely associated with Henry VIII.

The surrounding villages feature churches from the Saxon period, ancient bridges and water mills. Their communities are linked to Midhurst but retain a strong sense of independence.

Both the town and the villages are modern communities facing all the challenges of the modern world, whilst not losing sight of memories and customs from times gone by.

Our activities

- Commenting and advising on significant planning proposals
- Monitoring changes to listed buildings
- Supporting other local heritage groups
- Liaising with other local community groups to promote local heritage
- Liaising with local Councils and the National Park Authority
- High quality lecture programme and twice yearly magazine
- Campaigning on local issues
- Publishing books and other material of local interest

The challenges

We face a range of issues in protecting the cultural heritage of this special area, including planning proposals, housing developments, mineral extraction, large scale developments and, in Midhurst alone, protecting more than a hundred listed buildings. This can only happen with the involvement of the whole local community and an active heritage group.

Members

We welcome new members who share our aims and ideals. Application forms can be found at **www.midhurstsociety.org.uk**